Happy Holid...

Lunar New Year

by Betsy Rathburn

BLASTOFF! Beginners

BELLWETHER MEDIA
MINNEAPOLIS, MN

Blastoff! Beginners are developed by literacy experts and educators to meet the needs of early readers. These engaging informational texts support young children as they begin reading about their world. Through simple language and high frequency words paired with crisp, colorful photos, Blastoff! Beginners launch young readers into the universe of independent reading.

Blastoff! Universe

Reading Level | Grade K | Grades 1-3 | Grade 4

Sight Words in This Book 🔍

an	eat	in	of	their
and	get	is	out	they
are	has	it	people	with
day	have	many	red	
each	here	new	the	

This edition first published in 2023 by Bellwether Media, Inc.

No part of this publication may be reproduced in whole or in part without written permission of the publisher. For information regarding permission, write to Bellwether Media, Inc., Attention: Permissions Department, 6012 Blue Circle Drive, Minnetonka, MN 55343.

Library of Congress Cataloging-in-Publication Data

Names: Rathburn, Betsy, author.
Title: Lunar new year / by Betsy Rathburn.
Description: Minneapolis, MN : Bellwether Media, 2023. | Series: Happy holidays! | Includes bibliographical references and index. | Audience: Ages 4-7 | Audience: Grades K-1
Identifiers: LCCN 2022009284 (print) | LCCN 2022009285 (ebook) | ISBN 9781644876824 (library binding) | ISBN 9781648348587 (paperback) | ISBN 9781648347283 (ebook)
Subjects: LCSH: New Year--Juvenile literature. | Lunar calendars--Juvenile literature.
Classification: LCC GT4905 .R37 2023 (print) | LCC GT4905 (ebook) | DDC 394.2614--dc23/eng/20220224
LC record available at https://lccn.loc.gov/2022009284
LC ebook record available at https://lccn.loc.gov/2022009285

Editor: Christina Leaf   Designer: Laura Sowers

Printed in the United States of America, North Mankato, MN.

Table of Contents

It Is Lunar New Year!

The new moon is out.
Lunar New Year is here!

Fun Around the World

Lunar New Year is in January or February.

It lasts 15 days.
It ends with the
full moon.

full moon

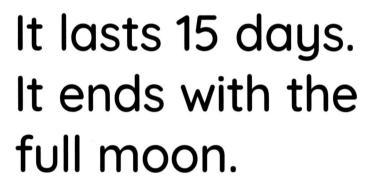

People around
the world enjoy it.
Many are in Asia.

Each year has
an animal.
The animals
have meanings.

Food and Fireworks

People clean
their houses.
They get rid of
bad luck.

People visit family.
They eat
dumplings
and rice balls.

dumplings

People watch **dragon dances.** They enjoy **fireworks.**

fireworks

dragon
dance

People give gifts.
Red **envelopes**
hold money.
Happy new year!

envelopes

Lunar New Year Facts

Celebrating Lunar New Year

dumplings

rice balls

envelope

Lunar New Year Activities

clean house

watch fireworks

give gifts

Glossary

dragon dances

dances where people move a long dragon puppet

dumplings

dough pockets that hold meat or vegetables

envelopes

folded papers used to hold things

fireworks

colorful blasts of light in the sky

To Learn More

ON THE WEB

FACTSURFER

Factsurfer.com gives you a safe, fun way to find more information.

1. Go to www.factsurfer.com.

2. Enter "Lunar New Year" into the search box and click 🔍.

3. Select your book cover to see a list of related content.

Index

The images in this book are reproduced through the courtesy of: wong yu liang, front cover; Makistock, p. 3; hxyume, pp. 4-5, 20-21; images by Tang Ming Tung/ Getty, pp. 6-7; Paitoon Pornsuksomboon, p. 8; Mcimage, pp. 8-9; domonite, pp. 10-11; PenWin, p. 12; atiger, pp. 12-13; PR Image Factory, pp. 14-15; Jiang Hongyan, pp. 16, 23 (dumplings); DragonImages/ Alamy, pp. 16-17; Chon Kit Leong, p. 18; windmoon, pp. 18-19, 23 (dragon dances); hareluya, p. 20; Alina Buzunova/ Alamy, p. 22; Prostock-studio, p. 22 (clean house); Tom Wang, pp. 22 (watch fireworks), 23 (envelopes); FamVeld, p. 22 (give gifts); Dana.S, p. 23 (fireworks).